# Life's BIG Little Moments

## GRANDMOTHERS & GRANDCHILDREN

# Life's BIG Little Moments

# GRANDMOTHERS & GRANDCHILDREN

SUSAN K. HOM

STERLING

New York / London
www.sterlingpublishing.com

For my grandmothers, with love

STERLING and the distinctive Sterling logo are registered trademarks of
Sterling Publishing Co., Inc.

Library of Congress Cataloging-in-Publication Data

Hom, Susan K.  Life's big little moments : grandmothers and grandchildren / Susan K. Hom.
        p. cm.
   ISBN-13: 978-1-4027-4318-4
   ISBN-10: 1-4027-4318-1
1.  Grandmothers--Miscellanea. 2.  Grandparent and child--Miscellanea.  I.
Title.
   HQ759.9.H66 2007  306.874'5--dc22

                                                        2007012383


10  9  8  7  6  5  4  3  2  1

Published by Sterling Publishing Co., Inc.
387 Park Avenue South, New York, NY 10016
Distributed in Canada by Sterling Publishing
c/o Canadian Manda Group, 165 Dufferin Street
Toronto, Ontario, Canada M6K 3H6
Distributed in the United Kingdom by GMC Distribution Services
Castle Place, 166 High Street, Lewes, East Sussex, England BN7 1XU
Distributed in Australia by Capricorn Link (Australia) Pty. Ltd.
P.O. Box 704, Windsor, NSW 2756, Australia

Printed in China

Sterling ISBN-13: 978-1-4027-4318-4
        ISBN-10: 1-4027-4318-1

For information about custom editions, special sales, premium and
corporate purchases, please contact Sterling Special Sales
Department at 800-805-5489 or specialsales@sterlingpub.com.

Cover and interior design by 3+Co. ( www.threeandco.com )

# Introduction

Whether it's while playing a game or on a trip to the zoo,
grandmothers equal fun. They are the best babysitters!
They tell funny stories about when they were young,
and they love to spoil their grandchildren.

Grandchildren add sweetness to everyday moments.
They are creative, lively, and spontaneous. They make silly faces
and laugh out loud, but can also be thoughtful and affectionate.
They offer an unexpected kiss or give a homemade card
that brightens a grandmother's day.

From ordinary to important moments, grandmothers
and grandchildren celebrate life's milestones together.
Grandmothers take delight in hearing their grandchildren say
their first words . . . and their wedding vows. In all of
life's BIG little moments, grandmothers and grandchildren
inspire each other to look for joy, magic, and love.

Grandmothers teach grandsons

**to hold on tightly.**

Grandsons encourage grandmothers

to spend the day barefoot.

Grandchildren
put their trust
in grandmothers.
Grandmothers pass
their wisdom along
to grandchildren.

Grandmothers introduce grandchildren

to the importance

of tradition.

Grandchildren make grandmothers

feel young again.

Grandchildren remind grandmothers

## how to fly a kite way up high.

Grandmothers show grandchildren

## how to plan a delightful picnic.

Grandmothers let grandchildren

**lick the batter off the spoon.**

Grandchildren show grandmothers

how to make everyday chores fun.

Grandchildren give grandmothers

**a high five.**

Grandmothers encourage grandchildren

to be curious.

Grandmothers rejoice

in seeing their grandsons

find happiness.

Grandsons make grandmothers

beam with pride.

Grandmothers help grandchildren

**explore the backyard.**

Grandchildren encourage grandmothers

to see familiar places

in new ways.

Grandmothers are

**proud of granddaughters.**

Granddaughters love

**when grandmothers
show them off.**

Grandmothers encourage grandchildren

to love reading.

Grandchildren show grandmothers

the best parts of

their favorite stories.

Grandmothers tell grandchildren

**that they are beautiful.**

Grandchildren remind grandmothers

that beauty is timeless.

Grandchildren inspire grandmothers

## to be open to new experiences.

Grandmothers introduce grandchildren

## to their family's history.

Grandmothers teach grandchildren

## how to play hide-and-seek.

Grandchildren show grandmothers

the best hiding places.

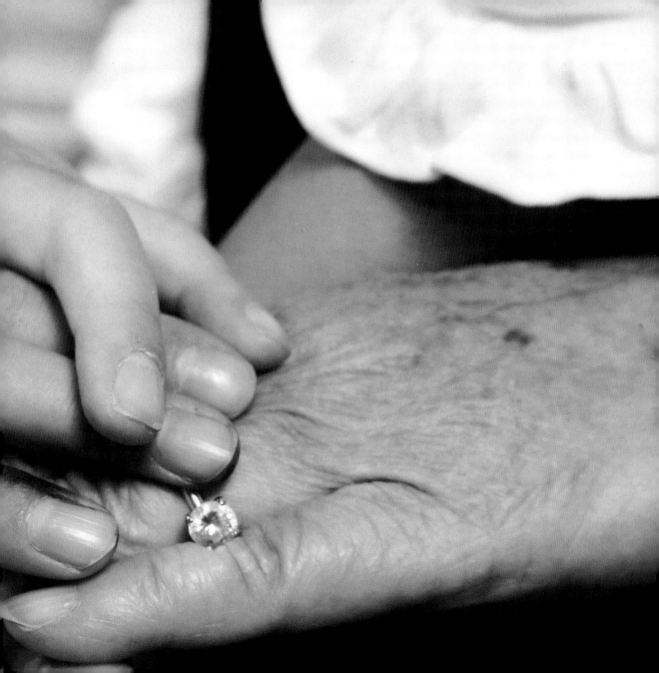

Grandchildren delight grandmothers

**with coos and bubbles.**

Grandmothers soothe grandchildren

with their favorite lullabies.

Grandmothers help grandchildren

**sound out difficult words.**

Grandchildren tell grandmothers

that they love

their time together.

Grandchildren remind grandmothers

to laugh out loud.

Grandmothers encourage grandchildren

to make silly noises.

Grandmothers love

## to spoil grandchildren
## on their birthdays.

Grandchildren spoil grandmothers

## with unconditional love.

Grandchildren enjoy

**being cuddled by**

**their grandmothers.**

Grandmothers whisper

"I love you" to grandchildren.

Grandmothers celebrate

grandchildren's birthdays

in style.

Grandchildren love to help

grandmothers with

the decorations.

Grandchildren beg grandmothers

**to read just one more book.**

Grandmothers encourage grandchildren

to snuggle close.

Grandmothers remind grandchildren

**to keep an open mind.**

Grandchildren inspire grandmothers to

make the most of every moment.

Grandsons prompt grandmothers

## to take lots of photos.

Grandmothers show grandsons

## pictures of their father as a baby.

Grandmothers encourage granddaughters

**to be generous.**

Granddaughters give

thoughtful gifts to grandmothers.

Grandchildren show grandmothers
how to wear sunglasses
like a movie star.
Grandmothers tell grandchildren
that they look fabulous.

Grandmothers know

**where grandchildren are ticklish.**

Grandchildren make grandmothers

feel like kids again.

Grandchildren show grandmothers

that no day is complete

without a good hug.

Grandmothers encourage grandchildren

to enjoy warm summer days.

Grandmothers reassure grandchildren
that small people can make
a big difference in the world.
Grandchildren remind grandmothers
to approach every task
with passion.

Grandchildren teach grandmothers

**to listen closely.**

Grandmothers help grandchildren

find the right words.

Grandchildren introduce grandmothers

## to new furry friends.

Grandmothers help grandchildren

## come up with the perfect name.

Grandsons inspire grandmothers

**to savor each moment.**

Grandmothers tell grandsons

that they are full of potential.

Grandmothers offer unlimited support

to grandchildren by going

to their recitals and games.

Grandchildren inspire grandmothers

to continue their hobbies.

Grandchildren show grandmothers

how to play their

favorite board games.

Grandmothers teach grandchildren

to win and lose gracefully.

Grandmothers help grandchildren

**discover their gifts.**

Grandchildren remind grandmothers

of the sweetness of childhood.

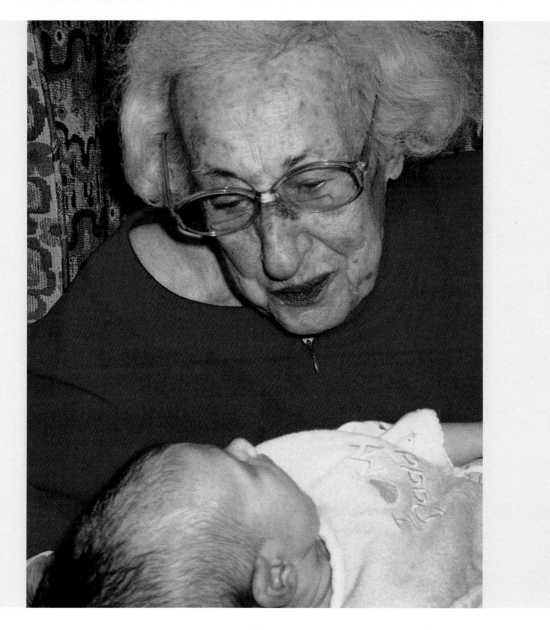

Grandchildren give grandmothers

**affectionate kisses.**

Grandmothers tell grandchildren

that they are precious.

Grandmothers encourage grandchildren

to appreciate gifts.

Grandchildren ask grandmothers

if they need any help.

Grandchildren

**confide in grandmothers.**

Grandmothers give

grandchildren helpful advice.

Grandmothers anticipate

**what grandchildren need.**

Grandchildren teach grandmothers

to be flexible.

Grandchildren ask grandmothers

"Why?"

Grandmothers help grandchildren

understand the world

around them.

Grandmothers encourage grandsons

**to smile.**

Grandsons fill grandmothers' days

with light and love.

Grandchildren remind grandmothers

## that there is wisdom in youth.

Grandmothers help grandchildren

## make smart decisions.

Grandmothers tell granddaughters
that they have the same eyes.
Granddaughters show grandmothers
that they also have the
same sense of humor.

Grandchildren inspire grandmothers

## to pet all kinds of animals.

Grandmothers remind grandchildren

## to be gentle.

Grandmothers

## cherish granddaughters.

Granddaughters love celebrating

precious days with

their grandmothers.

Grandchildren encourage grandmothers

## to be youthful.

Grandmothers inspire grandchildren

## to become wise.

Grandmothers inspire grandchildren

**to love others.**

Grandchildren help grandmothers

find magic in ordinary days.

# Photo Credits